Multi Biometric Thermal Face Recognition Using FWT and LDA Feature Extraction Methods with RBM DBN and FFNN Classifier Algorithms

Facial Recognition Using Thermal Imaging and Deep Belief Networks

Chigozie Orji
Evan Hurwitz

ELIVA PRESS

ELIVA PRESS

Chigozie Orji

Evan Hurwitz

Person recognition using thermal imaging, multi-biometric traits, with groups of feature filters and classifiers, is the subject of this paper. These were used to tackle the problems of biometric systems, such as a change in illumination and spoof attacks. Using a combination of, hard and soft-biometric, attributes in thermal facial images. The hard-biometric trait, of the shape of a head, was combined with soft-biometric traits such as the face wearing glasses, face wearing a cap/headgear, face with facial hairs, plain face, female face, and male face. These were experimented with, using images from Carl's database and Terravic Facial Infrared Database, and used to train clusters of neural network algorithms for each biometric trait. These comprised Restricted Boltzmann Machines (RBM), Deep Belief Networks (DBN), and Feed Forward Neural Networks (FFNN). After feature extraction, using Fast Wavelet Transform (FWT), and Linear Discriminant Analysis (LDA). A classification error of 0.02887, 0.038695, 0.02381, 0.024629, 0.0268, 0.02369 and 0.03 was achieved for each biometric trait, respectively. Showing that they had each been learned, and could be used through a fusion method, to improve recognition. This was demonstrated using a test image, as the user, having four of the character traits (countenance, glasses, facial hair, and gender). Then attempting to recognize each trait, one after the other, using a cross-verification method. The algorithm was seen to return test values, close to those received during the training test, for each biometric trait.

Published by Eliva Press SRL

Address: MD-2060, bd.Cuza-Voda, 1/4, of. 21 Chişinău, Republica
Moldova

Email: info@elivapress.com

Website: www.elivapress.com

ISBN: 978-1-63648-083-1

Contents

MULTI BIOMETRIC THERMAL FACE RECOGNITION USING FWT AND LDA FEATURE EXTRACTION METHODS WITH RBM DBN AND FFNN CLASSIFIER ALGORITHM

ABSTRACT

Person recognition using thermal imaging, multi-biometric traits, with groups of feature filters and classifiers, is the subject of this paper. These were used to tackle the problems of biometric systems, such as a change in illumination and spoof attacks. Using a combination of, hard and soft-biometric, attributes in thermal facial images. The hard-biometric trait, of the shape of a head, was combined with soft-biometric traits such as the face wearing glasses, face wearing a cap/headgear, face with facial hairs, plain face, female face, and male face. These were experimented with, using images from Carl's database and Terravic Facial Infrared Database, and used to train clusters of neural network algorithms for each biometric trait. These comprised Restricted Boltzmann Machines (RBM), Deep Belief Networks (DBN), and Feed Forward Neural Networks (FFNN). After feature extraction, using Fast Wavelet Transform (FWT), and Linear Discriminant Analysis (LDA). A classification error of 0.02887, 0.038695, 0.02381, 0.024629, 0.0268, 0.02369 and 0.03 was achieved for each biometric trait, respectively. Showing that they had each been learned, and could be used through a fusion method, to improve recognition. This was demonstrated using a test image, as the user, having four of the character traits (countenance, glasses, facial hair, and gender). Then attempting to recognize each trait, one after the other, using a cross-verification method. The algorithm was seen to return test values, close to those received during the training test, for each biometric trait.

1. INTRODUCTION

Thermal imaging is a preferable choice for facial biometrics because inconsistencies due to change in illumination are not present. The human body is luminous at frequencies, such as microwave, millimeter-wave and infrared. This makes it possible for thermal sensors to passively capture images of a consistent nature at these frequencies. Which are useful for biometric system applications such as person recognition [1]. Other frequencies, which are beyond Ultraviolet, are not suitable for such applications due to health-related issues such as genetic mutation and skin cancer, arising from their

1

prolonged exposure [2]. Figure 1 shows these frequency bands, highlighting the millimeter-wave band and that of visible light [3].

1.1. Person recognition

Person recognition has been an ever-growing work area, in visual sensor based biometrics. A field within which scientists and engineers are continually improving existing algorithms and developing new ones. These are useful in systems which detect, recognize and differentiate one type of person from the other. The following applications use biometrics with computer vision:

- Personal entertainment and assistance - Comprising video games, virtual reality, human-computer interaction, avatars, and robotics applications.
- Public enrollment and security - Some of which are driver's license, passport, voting, registration and enlistment programs. Along with welfare, identity document, passport, and voter forgery identification systems.
- Device access and authentication - Consisting of TV child proof locks, desktop access, personal device sign-in (mobile device and tablets), network and database authentication. Also internet access, online record and portal access (medical and law enforcement) with removable storage device access.
- Remote monitoring and surveillance - Such as advanced video surveillance and CCTV Control in airports (drug trafficking), malls and departmental stores (shoplifting). Also conference centers, cinemas, private premises, office buildings, and convenient stores.

This paper is an extension of the research work done by Evan, Ali and Chigozie [4]. It focuses on the appraisal of biometric system security and the proposal of a protection method, using thermal imaging and multi-biometric [5] traits to harden a biometric system through fusion [6]. Galbally, Marcel and Fierrez [7] discussed ways of fooling a biometric system into, passing an improper user as a legitimate one. By presenting a counterfeit crafted version of the genuine biometric trait to the sensor. Such as, 2D face spoofing using fake fingerprints, irises, photos, videos. Also 3D face spoofing using masks made of paper, plastic or silicone. Such spoofing methods, have been used to, compromise secure systems and reduce the confidence people have in biometrics. According to Hong, Jain and Pankanti [8] the integration of additional pieces of evidence, makes a biometric system more reliable and, increases verification accuracy.

Various approaches are possible, such as the integration of semblance and fingerprint, semblance and iris, and appearance and voice. For this research, additional evidence was created, using thermal images of *soft biometric* attributes, along with the *hard biometrics* of the human face. A technique which doesn't require, the use of, multiple sensor input devices to increase robustness. The weaknesses that can exist in a recognition system arise from a hacker's awareness of the biometric information required for user authentication and his ability to falsify them. The use of hidden, authentication, evidence improves a system's robustness and hardens it against such attacks. All possible combinations, of biometric attributes, have not been exhausted. That is why the work in this research is focused on, multi-biometric person recognition, using soft and *hard biometric* traits in thermal facial images. Using a matching score and fusion approach, to combine biometric evidence and altogether boost security.

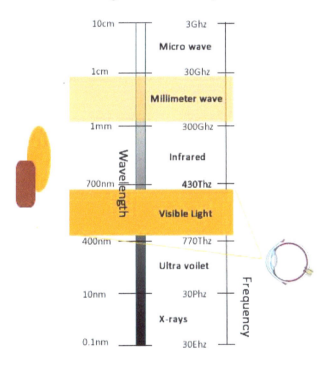

Figure 1: Imaging beyond the visible spectrum, showing the optical eye, using visible light frequencies, and thermal sensor device, using millimeter-wave frequencies

1.2. Data sets

The availability of datasets helped to further motivate the research initiative. These comprised images of different types of people captured under diverse conditions such as poses, lighting, dressing, and makeup. From these samples, for training and testing the anti-spoof algorithm to achieve reduced vulnerability, were derived. The Object Tracking and Classification Beyond the Visible Spectrum (OTCBVS) benchmark dataset collection [9], and Carl's databases [10], have provided a dataset of images, captured under diverse conditions, using thermal imaging. Which can help research work in the area of person recognition. The facial category, within the OTCBVS benchmark dataset collection: Terravic Facial IR Database, provides thermal facial images with good variability. These comprise real-life shots having diverse behavioral characteristics. While Carl's database consists of real-life facial images, captured simultaneously, using visible and invisible frequencies. They have gender variation and good behavioral attributes. Both datasets, comprise ideal thermal facial human categories and, are suitable for measuring the working of a multi-biometric person recognition system.

2. LITERATURE REVIEW

Biometrics is the science of knowing a person's identity, using thier physical or behavioral qualities, such as the semblance, fingerprints, voice, and iris [11]. The idea, that spurred biometrics as a science, was introduced within the field of law enforcement. When Alphonse Bertillon, police head of the criminal identification department in Paris, introduced a new way to identify criminals. Using using body measurements such as eye color, skin, hair, beard, fingers, shape, and size of the head, [12].

A classical biometric system can verify identity by:

- Capturing biometric information such as images, fingerprint and voice samples from people.

- Extract features from the information.

- Match the feature set against feature patterns in the database.

- Conclude an identity verification.

Aside from verification, information collected by a biometric algorithm can be used to ascertain additional peculiarities of the persons concerned. Traits such as hair, gender, gait, age, clothing, ethnicity, and body weight can be captured [13]. This additional data can help in bettering recognition verity in a biometric algorithm [14].

Biometrics also saw application in the field of legal work such as criminal identification and illegal migrant monitoring. It is also useful for security clearances among employees in sensitive occupations, forensics, the identification of prisoners among suspects and ex-convicts. In today's world the private sector, comprising of civilians, is beginning to add biometrics to alphanumeric methods, for person recognition [15].

2.1. Biometrics systems

A biometric system can be used for recognizing persons using the recognition of patterns in a feature vector. These can be derived from a particular corporal or behavioral attribute that the individual possesses. Depending on the type of application a biometric system works either in *verification* or *identification mode* [16].

2.2. Biometric system errors

Multiple samples of simmilar biometric attribute, retrieved from one individual, are not always alike. Such as two exposures of a person's face, two prints of a person's left index finger and two voice samples from the same person. Effects such as changes in the user's physiology, caused by wounds, cuts, unusual dressing, moods, ambient lighting, weather, and age, can cause errors in a biometric system. The user's way of interacting with the sensor can have the same effect. As a result a matching score, in numerical terms, is used to describe the similtude between the input (captured biometric trait) and database template. Such that, the higher the score the more convinced the system is that, the two biometric data come from the same user. The system's decision is regulated by a threshold "s", for the matching score, such that the higher the "s" the more secure the system. A biometric verification system can make, two kinds of errors, a false accept (false match) or a false reject (false nonmatch) [17]

2.3. Hard and Soft biometrics

A person's image, normally, comprises both hard and soft-biometric characteristics [18]. Some hard-biometric characteristics are countenance, the shape of the head and gait. While soft-biometric characteristics are features such as glasses, hair, hat, clothes, gender and other occlusions that an individual may have on.

2.3.1. Hard-biometrics

Memory-based authentication methods, such as usernames and passwords, can easily be compromised if written down in plain text and such text files are copied. Such authentication systems can be hardened by capturing and verifying a hard biometric trait along with the alphanumeric information. Hard biometric methods are more dependable than alphanumeric authentication schemes. They also have several advantages that alphanumeric methods do not grant. Hard biometric authentication involves the establishment of a person's identity with, the use of physical characteristics. These are traits such as the face, iris, fingerprint, hand geometry, gait, voice, etc. Unlike alphanumeric tokens, Hard biometric traits cannot be copied, shared or distributed, they can also neither be lost or forgotten. Hard biometrics always requires that the person, being validated, be present at the time and place where access is being requested. Hard biometric traits are arduous to forge and a lot of money, time, access and experience, would be needed to forge them. For application-specific use each hard biometric trait has its advantages and disadvantages. The type of use, however, derives from the application requiring it. ATMs would use facial biometric traits, video surveillance: gait, while telebanking and telemarketing would use voice.

2.3.2. Soft-biometrics

Semantics, in the context of person recognition, are characteristics which people often use in describing those they meet but don't know personally. Such as stature, gender, skin color, hair color, body weight, age, race, facial features, mode of dressing and mannerisms [19]. Using such semantic data, with features from a biometric dataset, to further enhance the working of a person recognition algorithm, is called "soft-biometrics". It bears with it all the advantages of the hard-biometric authentication schemes, over alphanumeric methods, and can be used to further harden hard-biometric methods against spoofing. Reid and Nixon [14] attribute this to the use of labels and measurements, which take the appearance of mere human depictions, that people can easily grasp. Samangooei, Guo, Mark, and Nixon [20] define these as semantic annotations. Dantcheva, Velardo, D'Angelo and Dugelay [21] present a novel definition for soft-biometrics based on additional biometric traits. Some of which are: color of clothes, material accessories, body weight, physical and behavioral traits. Jain, Dass, and

Nandakumar [22] describe soft-biometrics as being able to provide information about an individual but without the ability to create a full distinction between that individual and others [23].

3. RELATED WORK

Taking a lead from a paper on thermal facial recognition [24] and other works which use soft biometrics to augment hard biometric methods [25], [14]. A contemporary approach, to person recognition, using thermal imaging is being proposed. With a focus on facial data, hard and soft biometric attributes [4]. Most person recognition systems, depending on the operating environment and scenario, have to choose sensor type. Also, based on the sensing setup and output, have to choose a prediction approach. Irrespective of these, the following steps are common to most systems:

- Detection.
- Feature extraction.
- Semantic analysis.
- Feature matching.
- Recognition result.

Most systems begin with detecting a biometric aspect required for recognition such as head, gait, face, finger, and iris. Then separating it from the rest of the image. This step, which is the detection (data acquisition and pre-processing) step, is an integral part of the sensor device setup. It requires a lot of accuracy and is not always discussed. As the performance of the subsequent steps and the system as a whole, depend on it. As a result of the technicalities involved in the first step, the focus of this research project would begin with the second step. Which is about feature extraction. This chapter attempts to present an overview, of the work that has been done in the field of person recognition over the past few years, focusing on the techniques and algorithms used.

3.1. Person Recognition Methods

Experiments were done by, Bhattacharjee, Seal, Ganguly, Nasipuri, and Basu, with the Terravic Facial IR Database. Using Haar wavelet transform and Local Binary Pattern (LBP) [24]. Martinez, Binefa, and Pantic propose recognition, in thermal images, using the detection of the eyes, nostrils and mouth. Also the subsequent decomposition into a feature vector with Haar wavelets, and classification using SVM and Gentle boost [26]. Herrmann, Müller, Willersinn, and Beyerer achieved an error rate reduction, of up to 80% on Long Wave Infrared (LWIR) images, using the AMROS and OTCBVS benchmark datasets. The achieved detection, using Maximally Stable Extremal Regions (MSER), and classification with a Convolutional Neural Network (CNN) [27]. For deep learning Krizhevsky, Sutskever, and Hinton used non-saturating neurons and a GPU implementation of CNN to classify 1.2 million high-resolution images [28]. Shangfei et al. worked on a Natural Visible and thermal Infrared facial Expression database (NVIE). Using expression recognition and emotion inference for 100 subjects with and without glasses. They analyzed with Principle Component Analysis (PCA), Linear Discriminant Analysis (LDA), and the Active Appearance Model (AAM) [29]. Kelly, Stefanie, and Tom did a study on, alternate access methods using, infrared sensing, electromyography, oculography, and computer vision for individuals with severe motor impairments [30]. Bhowmik et al. researched the advantages, of thermal face over visible face, for recognition, using IRIS and the Terravic Facial IR Database. They isolated the various IR spectrums, showing the Long Wave Infrared (LWIR) band, as that with the highest emissions and suitability for face recognition. They compared this to Short Wave Infrared (SWIR) and Medium Wavelength Infrared (MWIR) [31]. Ayan, Suranjan, Debotosh, Mita and Dipak Kumar proposed the use of Thermal Minutiae Points (TMP), using blood perfusion data as a feature, for thermal face recognition. They experimented with PCA, LDA, and Equinox, for feature extraction and a multi-layer perceptron back propagation feed-forward neural network for feature classification and recognition of thermal infrared face images [32]. Siu-Yeung, Lingyu, and Wen proposed, using the Modified Hausdorff Distance, to measure the similarity between two feature vectors of thermal faces [33]. Ognjen, Riad and Roberto worked on, improving recognition in visible and, thermal images through the detection of prescription glasses [34].

3.1.1. Background subtraction

This person detection method assumes an image to be part of a continuous stream of pictures and attempts to predict the type of background using the frame sequence in the time domain. A comprehensive overview of the method has been done by Piccardi [35]. The method, however, has a problem with, shadow effects, sudden changes in illumination, occlusions and, scenes within which a person remains static for a long time. These problems can be ameliorated by, equipping cameras with, ground analysis capability [36], thermal imaging and stereo capabilities [37].

Here is a list of background subtraction methods:

• Running Gaussian average
• Temporal median filter

- Mixture of Gaussians
- Kernel density estimation (KDE)
- Sequential KD approximation
- Co-occurrence of image variations
- *Eigen backgrounds*

3.1.2. Silhouette

This method involves creating the silhouette of an image through binarization [25], using its edges and contours, and matching it with prior
models in the persons' database [38]. This method works well for detecting people, using facial images showing countenance, not wearing occlusions or having unique behavioral attributes [39]. The detection of partially occluded persons, was tackled by Wu and Nevatia, by breaking down the image into segments they called edgelets. Then the learning of the features, of each segment, by an AdaBoost algorithm. Then compiling prediction results, made for each segment, to ascertain overall detection accuracy [40].

3.1.3. Appearance, look and feel

This method models the image, based on its appearance and attempts to extract features from it, using the look and feel of the many surfaces that make it up. The features are used to train a classifier algorithm, which learns its various attributes and is able, to make predictions on new images based on the feature set. The method can be used, based on the whole image or, by using bits of the image and summing up the learned features.

3.2. The Whole Image Approach

A novel way of achieving this is, by using wavelets, to analyze the whole image, at a pixel level and computing the difference between the different areas. Some known wavelet transform methods are Continuous Wavelet Transform (CWT), Gabor Wavelet Transform (GWT), Discrete Wavelet Transform (DWT), Haar's Wavelet Transform (HWT) and Fast Wavelet Transform (FWT) [41]. The first known one was DWT invented by, a Hungarian mathematician, Alfréd Haar in 1909.

Fourier transform is also useful for this type of analysis. Its weakness is that it doesn't account for the spatial information only the frequency aspects. These approaches are good for, extracting features from, thermal facial images. Bhattacharjee, Seal, Ganguly, Nasipuri, and Basu used the HWT method, with a Local Binary Patterns (LBP) classifier, to process cropped thermal faces. Divided into frequency bands LL1, LH1, HL1, HH1, where LL1 corresponds to, the lowest frequency band and HH1, the highest frequency band [25]. Figure 5 shows a sketch map, of the wavelet bands from a thermal face, after quadratic wavelet decomposition.

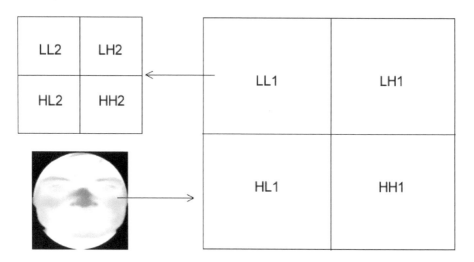

Figure 2: Sketch map of wavelet bands, after quadratic wavelet decomposition of a thermal facial image, showing low and high-frequency areas and sub-bands within the LL1 band [25].

Jones, Viola, and Snow used the wavelet technique, with motion and appearance information, to detect walking people, for outdoor surveillance. After which they classified, them, using a cascaded AdaBoost classifier [42]. For detecting walking people, Zhu, Yeh, Cheng, and Avidan used the Histogram of Oriented Gradients (HOGs) technique. They applied a cascade of rejectors approach using a weak AdaBoost classifier. Using their method, they were able to reduce computation time [43].

3.3. The Part Image Approach

This approach processes images, by detecting their aspects for person recognition, and decides by combining the various classifications. For full-body images the head, hands, legs, and torso, are detected separately, processed, and classified. Mohan, Papageorgiou, and Poggio worked on detecting people, in cluttered scenes, using an Adaptive Combination of Classifiers (ACC). The method first uses a four-part, detector, separately trained, to detect four segments of the human body, namely: head, legs, right arm, and left arm. After the body parts have been detected, a subsequent classifier is used to classify the results of the four patterns, as a person or nonperson [44].

Wu and Nevatia worked on detecting, partially occluded, humans within video streams. They used part detectors, and weak classifiers, based on features they called edgelets [45]. Their method involved using face, eyes, nose, ears, and mouth separately, before processing and classifying. Trujillo, Olague, Hammoud, and Hernandez experimented with the IRIS data-set. They combined facial feature localization, with the holistic approach using clustering, Eigenface feature extraction and SVM for classification [46].

Martinez, Binefa, and Pantic focused on detecting, facial components (eyes, nostrils, and mouth) in thermal images, using Haar features with GentleBoost algorithm [47]. Al-Khalidi, Saatchi, Burke, and Elphick developed an approach, for tracking a Region of Interest (ROI) on the human face, using thermal video images. The ROI: tip of the nose was tracked using warm and cold facial points of the human face [48].

3.4. History of biometric recognition

Ever since the beginning people have used bodily attributes such as voice, hair, face, and gait, to recognize one another. The idea, that spurred biometrics as a science, was introduced within the field of law enforcement. Its inception was towards the end of the 19th century. When Alphonse Bertillon, police head of the criminal identification department in Paris, introduced the idea of using body measurements, such as skin, eye color, hair, beard, fingers, size, and shape of the head, to identify criminals [11]. This was followed by, a second finding within the same field of law enforcement. The discovery of how human fingerprints are distinct from each other. After which many law-enforcement bureaus began the practice of booking offenders by fingerprinting. The fingerprint data was stored in card files which were replaced by databases. In the hands of law enforcement this method was further improved for determining criminal identities. By using the ability to match fingerprint fragments, from crime scenes, with those in the criminal's database. Beyond law-enforcement biometrics also saw initial application in legal work. Such as in criminal identification, illegal migrant identification, security clearances among employees in sensitive occupations and forensics. Also the identification of ex-convicts, prisoners among suspects, paternal and maternal determinations and much more. In today's world, the private sector, comprising civilians is beginning to include biometrics to alphanumeric methods for person recognition [49].

3.4.2. Verification mode

In verification mode a biometric scheme confirms an individual's identity, by comparing the received biometric characteristic, with the owner's biometric template captured in its database. Such systems work by using the assertion of one who is seeking access to perform a one to one comparison and return a true or false. This is done using a Personal Identification Number (PIN) code, an alphanumeric code, a bar code, a login name or smart card.

3.4.3. Identification mode

In identification mode the scheme recognizes, a person's identity, by searching the template database for a match. This is done with received biometric characteristic after comparing the input to many records in the database. The check either passes, when a match is found, or declines if the person is not enrolled in the system's database. The Identification mode is also used for negative recognition. This entails the system determining that a person is who he or she denies being. This is useful in a situation that a person attempts to use multiple or stolen identities. Negative recognition can however only be used with biometrics. Passwords, keys, tokens, and PINs, can only serve for positive recognition.

3.4.4. A false accept

A false accept, also known as a false match, is the confusion of biometric samples from two different users to be, from one person. For a biometric scheme it is represented numerically as the False Match Rate (FMR).

3.4.5. A false reject

A false reject, also construed as a false nonmatch, is the mistaking of two biometric samples from the same user to be from two different individuals. For a system it is represented numerically as the False Non-Match Rate (FNMR). Besides recognition error rates: FMR and FNMR, other parameters which help to sum up a biometric system's performance are the Failure to Capture (FTC) and Failure to Enroll (FTE) rates [50].

3.4.6. The Failure to Capture rate

FTC rate is the number of times, in percentage, the biometric device is unable to capture a sample when users present their biometric attribute.

3.4.7. The Failure to Enroll rate

FTE rate is the number of occasions, in percentage, users are unable to enlist in the recognition scheme. This could be because of a network issue, a system issue or an issue with the sensor, during biometric characteristic capturing.

3.5. Hard-biometrics

A person's image, normally, comprises both hard and soft biometric characteristics. The hard biometric characteristics are - face, iris, and gait. The soft biometric characteristics are - gender, hair, hat, clothes with other occlusions that the individual may have on [51].

3.5.1. Face

This is a commonly used and nonintrusive biometric trait. Its application ranges from authentication in a static fixed background, to one in a dynamic and changing environment. A method used in face recognition involves; 1) the identification of, Regions of Interest (ROI) such as, eyes, eyebrows, nose, lips, and chin and the analysis of their spatial relationship; 2) another is total analysis, of all images that constitute a face, using a weighted aggregate of several model faces, to develop face space and the location of new images within face space. The challenge, with face recognition, is the capturing process. A fixed and simple background, with known illumination type, is often assumed. However, it is not always the case. A Facial Recognition System (FRS) should be able to automatically; 1) Detect the presence of a face within captured images; 2) Locate the face; 3) Recognize the face [52]. The use of a thermal sensor, good feature extraction methods, with deep learning algorithms, would surmount the challenges and increase the capabilities of the system.

3.5.2. Iris

The Iris is the portion of the eye between the pupil and the white of the eye (sclera). Its complex patterns, carry distinct information per individual and, are useful for person recognition. The irises of all persons, even of identical twins, are expected to differ. Iris systems have low *False Accept Rate (FAR)* however their *False Reject Rate (FRR)* can be high [53].

3.5.3. Fingerprint

Fingerprints have been used, for decades, for personal identification. It dates back, to the origin of biometrics, as one of the first methods used for enrolling and documenting human beings. A fingerprint is peculiar for every person. It comprises a unique arrangement of ridges and valleys on the finger surface. For large scale identification, covering millions, an enrolment system comprising multiple fingerprints (all five fingers), from each person, would be more robust than one based on single fingers. However genetic factors, with aging and job-related issues (e.g., motor mechanics, farmers, bricklayers, and manual laborers), affect the general use of fingerprint for automatic identification.

3.5.4. Hand geometry

This recognition approach is based on dimensions of the human palm its length, width, shape, and size. Hand geometry is not affected by manual labor, work factors, or environmental factors, such as heat or humidity. It is however not very distinctive, and in a large population, more than one person could have the same hand geometry. Also factors such as physical impairment, lack of motor function, paralysis and arthritis, affect the universal use of hand geometry for automatic authentication.

3.5.5. Gait

Gait biometrics, is an appearance-based authentication   method, which works well with video sequences. The ubiquity of video cameras has made this type of recognition popular. Gait biometrics, is quite distinctive and, can serve for automatic recognition among persons in a large population. It is very useful for recognition over distances, and under poor resolution conditions, but is affected by factors such as fast-changing backgrounds, occlusions, costumes and differences in lighting.

3.5.6. Voice

Voice recognition comprises both hard and soft biometrics. The *hard biometrics* being aspects such as, the mouth, vocal cavity, vocal tracts and lips. While the *soft biometrics* consist of emotional states such as age, health conditions, etc. Voice is not very distinguishing, and would not be useful for automatic recognition, among persons in a large population. A voice recognition scheme may be text-independent or text-dependent. The text-independent types, being more arduous to design than text-dependent ones and, offering better security. Voice is also affected by environmental influence such as noise and echo.

3.6. Hybrid systems

These systems merge *soft biometric* data, with *hard biometric* information, to increase overall accuracy. Described by Jain, Dass, and Nandakumar, it suggests the complementing of primary biometric information gathered from fingerprint and face with *soft biometric* data, to achieve resistance to circumvention acceptability, collectability, permanence, universality and distinctiveness [54]. Scheirer, Kumar, Ricanek, Belhumeur and Boult referred to this as, improving match scores from, face recognition attempts resulting from incomplete measurements done at match time. By using Bayesian Attributes Networks to combine descriptive attributes, such as *soft biometrics,* with primary biometric observations [55]. Also the use of multi-biometrics, comprising soft and hard biometrics, in a recognition system helps in hardening it against unwanted error rates and spoof attacks (such as fraudsters attempting to forge an identity). It also helps, in the case of insufficient population coverage, where little is known about most candidates monitored, using a recognition system [56].

4. THE PROPOSED METHOD

The method was researched using thermal facial replicas from the Terravic Facial Infrared Database [9] and Carl's database [10]. These were processed using the Large Time-Frequency Analysis Toolbox (LTFAT) in Octave [57] for FWT and Byte fish face recognition toolbox [58] was used for facial image set importation tools. Rasmus Berg Palm's deep learning toolbox [59], was used for, Restricted Boltzmann Machines (RBM), Deep Belief Network (DBN) and Feed Forward Neural Network (FFNN) algorithms. Figure 3 shows a schematic of the proposed system's structure.

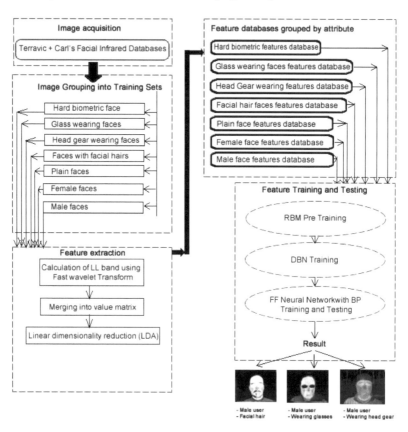

Figure 3: The proposed system, for multi-biometric thermal face recognition, using FWT image compression approach, LDA feature extractor, and RBM, DBN with FFNN classifiers.

4.1. The Terravic Infrared Database

     This is one of the two openly usable thermal face image databases. The other is IRIS (Imaging, Robotics and Intelligent System) Thermal/Visible Face Database. It is a subset of the OTCBVS benchmark and is good for experiments in the area of computer vision algorithms. Along with *hard* and *soft biometric* detection using thermal images. The data set comprises thermal sequences of 20 different people, each sequence having variations such as, right, left, front, outdoor, indoor, hat and glasses. All captured, with a Thermal-Eye 2000AS Raytheon L-3 sensor, with a focus on facial analysis for thermal imagery. The images have an 8-bit grayscale with, JPEG format, each one being 320 x 240 pixel in size [8]. Four independent training sets, having *soft biometric* attributes, were established from the dataset. Case study images from each one are presented in Figure 4, Figure 5, Figure 6 and Figure 7.

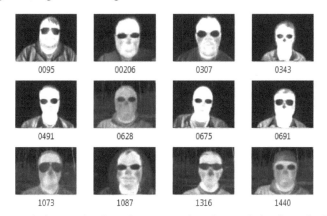

Figure 4: Case study images having glasses-wearing charateristic, from the Terravic Facial Infrared Database.

Figure 5: Case study images having headgear charateristic, from the Terravic Facial Infrared Database.

Figure 6: Case study images having facial hair charateristic, from the Terravic Facial Infrared Database.

Figure 7: Case study images having plain face charateristic, from the Terravic Facial Infrared Database.

4.2. Fast Wavelet Transform (FWT)

Thermal images, which are a mixture of mixed and relevant detail, can be filtered using a wavelet transform technique. This breaks down the image into regions of high and low-frequency comprising frequency and spatial components, through a compression technique. Graphically these can be represented as sub-bands. Some common wavelet transform approaches are Fast Wavelet Transform, Discrete Wavelet Transform, Gabor Wavelet Transform and Continuous Wavelet Transform [60]. Fast Wavelet Transform (FWT) was used with Octave, in the experiments, because of its application to thermal facial imaging [61]. FWT is a constituent of the Large Time-Frequency Analysis Toolbox (LTFAT) [62].

4.3. Linear Discriminant Analysis (LDA)

LDA accomplishes the derivation of points of highest variance, from images in feature space. It does this by making sure the within-class distance (S_w) is less, for images in the same class and between class distance (S_b) more, for images in seperate classes. It advances the Principal Component Analysis (PCA) [63] method, through the way it derives the covariance matrices, applying linear discriminants [64].

$$AV = \lambda Y \tag{1}$$

Where $A = Covariance\ matrix$, $V = Eigenvector$,
λ = Diagonal matrix of analogous Eigen values.

$$S_b V = \lambda S_w V \tag{2}$$

Where, $V = The\ eigenvector$, $\lambda = Eigen\ values$.

4.4. Restricted Boltzmann Machines

Deep-belief networks are constituted using simple dual-layer neural networks called RBMs. Their layer design comprises both visible and hidden layers. Having same layer nodes restricted from communicating and different layer nodes allowed to communicate. Each node being a standalone center for data processing. Accepting its input and randomly choosing whether to transmit that input or not. Some applications of the RBM algorithm being regression, feature learning, classification, dimensionality reduction, topic modeling and collaborative filtering [65].

$$f((x*w)+b)= a \qquad (3)$$

Where, $x= Input,\ w= Weights, b= Bias, f= Activation\ function, a= Output.$

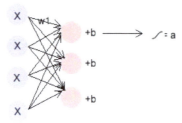

Figure 8: RBM network depicting *inputs x*, *weight w1* for a connected node, bias for hidden layer and outputed activation function.

4.5. Deep Belief Networks (DBN)

When two RBM layers constitute a network, with many hidden layers, they become a Deep Belief Network (DBN). With this structure DBNs are able to learn highly structured data, such as thermal images. The irregular layer design of the RBM, makes its input to propagate through Contrastive Divergence, such that good classification is achieved irrespective of network depth. Using an unsupervised algorithm, the RBM is first pre-trained. After which the error received at the output, is sent to the input through backpropagation. After which supervised learning begins, by adjusting the weights on the successive forward pass [66]. The expected outcome is to reconstruct a target vector, using a speculative approach, with as little inaccuracy as possible. This is done, after several forward and back passes. Tools from Rasmus Berg Palm's deep learning toolbox, for RBM and DBN, have been used [59].

Table 1: Deep Belief Network Architecture

Feature	Description
Activation function	Sigmoid
Input Layer	1
Output Layer	1
Momentum	0
Alpha	1
Batch scope	10
Epochs	100
RBM start-up weight	100 by 784 zero matrix
RBM unit scope	100 layers
DBN start-up weights	100 by 784 zero matrix
DBN scope	100 by 100 RBM units

The Deep Belief Net design comprises an RBM having 100 hidden layers and a DBN consisting of 100 by 100 RBM units. The RBM algorithm weights were used to commence the Deep Belief Network after pre-training with 10 epochs of 100 batches each. Using different start-up seeds, the DBN algorithm was trained many times, for each concourse. Running 100 batches per epoch, the DBN algorithm completed 10 epochs, for each *soft-biometric* class. After which the number of iterations was plotted against the average reconstruction error. An error of 0.026% was achieved for plain faces, 6.05% for glass faces, 0.026% for head gear faces, and 0.026% for

facial hair faces. A feed-forward neural network classifier was initialized using the final DBN weights. Here is the DBN architecture.

4.6. Feed Forward Neural Network

A FFNN has been applied, as the secondary classifier, for the algorithm. After target vector reconstruction, the DBN, was spread out into a FFNN. This was trained by applying 10 epochs of 100 batches respectively and used to classify sample images from the *soft-biometric* groups.

4.7. Training data acquisition

To design the biometric system, sample images were acquired using public and private thermal facial datasets, namely: the Terravic Facial Infrared Database [9] and Carl's database [10]. The former was used in learning soft and hard-biometric attributes, while the latter for gender attributes, of female and male.

4.8. Image pre-processing and feature extraction

The behavioral and physical attributes of persons, under low lighting conditions can be ascertained, using thermal imaging. Behavioral (outward) attributes such as cap, glasses, hat and facial hair with physical attributes such as head shape and size can be used to classify persons and afterwards recognize them. For thermal imaging a sturdy feature extraction method is requisite. Firstly, Fast Wavelet Transform (FWT), for filtering the noise from the thermal images and secondly, Linear Discriminant Analysis (LDA), for extracting their principal components.

4.9. The multi-biometric recognition method

Using images from the Terravic Facial Infrared Database, the hard-biometric trait (shape of a head) along with *soft-biometric* traits (glasses, a cap, a mustache, beard or gender) will be detected from a single image. Using a single thermal sensor with matching algorithms trained to recognize each feature. After which the outcome of each match would be, fused and, used to make the final decision. This is illustrated in Figure 9.

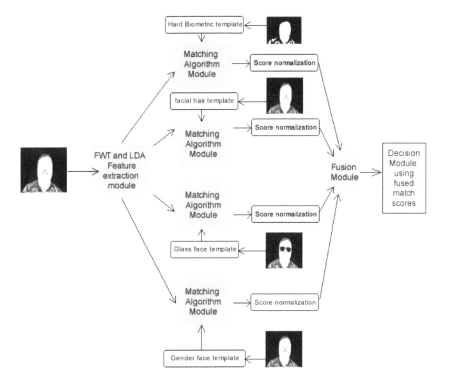

Figure 9: Proposed multi-biometric person recognition system, with single sensor thermal imaging, using a *parallel mode* of operation, with the score fusion approach, for soft and *hard biometric* traits; images from the Terravic Facial Infrared Database.

4.9.1. Multi-biometric recognition modes

To implement multi-biometrics a system can function using any of these three diverse modes of operation, namely: 1) The *serial mode*; 2) The *parallel mode* and; 3) The *hierarchical mode* [64].

4.9.1.1. The serial mode

Operating in the serial mode, the recognition result gathered from verifying the first trait, is used to reduce the scope of possible matches. The same is done, with subsequent traits, until a final trait is used, to complete the matching process.

4.9.1.2. Parallel

Operating in the *parallel mode*, recognition time is reduced by verifying all the traits concurrently, then using a fusion approach, to sum the matching scores from each search. After which, the result is measured against a threshold score *"s"* before, a final decision is made.

4.9.1.3. Hierarchical

In the *hierarchical mode* of operation, results from respective classifiers, for each biometric evidence, are combined using a staggered, trait by trait, approach with the decision made after a final fusion stage.

4.9.2. Types of multi-biometric fusion

In a *multi-biometric* recognition system's evidence can be combined, before or after the matching process, using different schemes, some of which are: 1) A *sensor level* scheme; 2) A *feature level* scheme; 3) A *match score level* scheme and; 4) A *decision level* scheme [67]. Figure 9 shows a schematic of the proposed multi-biometric system, comprising several matching algorithms and a fusion module before decision, using the fused match scores.

4.9.2.1. The sensor level fusion scheme

This applies to a *multi-sensor* system. It works with *fusion* at the unprocessed data level, using the inputs from each sensor. The received traits are combined to form a single trait, from which features are extracted. An example, for face biometrics, is a system that combine inputs from visible, near-Infrared and thermal spectrum sensors [10].

4.9.2.2. The feature level scheme

This method fuses processed features, from each biometric trait, into a final feature set with which the person is recognized. An example is the fusion of facial linear discriminants, from images of the shape of a user's head, with a *soft-biometric* trait such as gender [68]. To form a single feature set with which a user can be recognized.

Table 2: Matching Algorithm With Score Fusion Method

Matching algorithm with the input image to the left	Score
Facial hair features Hard biometric features Test to confirm facial hair features belong to hard biometric user	Score 1, if the hard-biometric features in the input image belong to the authentic user (with facial hair). Score 0 if they do not.
Facial hair features Glass face features Test to confirm facial hair features belong to glass face user	Score 1, if the glass wearing features in the input image belong to the authentic user (with facial hair). Score 0 if they do not.
Facial hair features Male gender face features Test to confirm facial hair features belong to male gender user	Score 1 if the male gender features in the input image belong to the authentic user (with facial hair). Score 0 if they do not.
Total score	3

4.9.2.3. The match level scheme

This method sums up, numerical, scores outputted from each classifier. The sum is used, to make the final decision, based on comparison to a threshold score *s*. An example is matching scores from verifying different *soft-biometric* traits such as, particular head shape, the presence of facial hair, glasses or male gender, as shown in Figure 9. Table 2 below illustrates the *match level* scheme with *score fusion*.

4.9.2.4. The decision level scheme

This is a voting scheme in which each classifier makes its own decision after verifying the biometric trait presented to it. All the votes are presented at the output. A majority of positive votes indicate an identity as verified. While negative votes indicate an identity as unverified.

4.10. The approach

The single thermal imaging sensor approach, proposed here, will use the *parallel mode* of operation, as shown in Figure 9 with the matching classifier algorithms shown in Figure 3. It will reduce biometric system errors, by working as a hybrid system in verification mode, using the whole image approach for face biometrics. By having each algorithmic cluster, verify a particular feature trait and, yield a matching score. Then use the *match level* scheme, to make its final decision, through score fusion, as shown in Table 2.

The matching algorithms will each comprise, Fast Wavelet Transform (FWT) and Linear Discriminant Analysis (LDA) for preprocessing, the removal of noise and retrieval of the spatial, time-frequency components. The isolation of the principal components of each image would be done using LDA. The pre-processed feature set will each be classified using, an ensemble of Restricted Boltzmann Machines (RBM) algorithms, Deep Belief Network (DBN) algorithms and Feed Forward Neural Network (FFNN) algorithms. For verifying, each feature trait, and yielding a matching score, for final decision making through score fusion.

5. Experiment One: Image Pre-processing and Feature Extraction.

These facial recognition experiments were conducted, for *hard* and *soft-biometric* thermal images, using FWT and Linear Discriminant Analysis (LDA) for feature extraction. FWT is part of the Large Time-Frequency Analysis Toolbox (LTFAT) and is available as a package in GNU Octave.

5.1. Hard-biometrics

The image processing was first done to extract the hard biometric traits from the facial images. This was achieved by image binarization, using octave, to retrieve the shape of the head from each of the images.

5.1.1. Image binarization

This was done using a threshold technique, to determine the head size and shape. It was applied for extracting the hard-biometric attribute of the thermal images. The technique is a common pre-processor used in OCR (Optical Character Recognition), and is useful in pattern recognition, for exposing the uniqueness of an image.

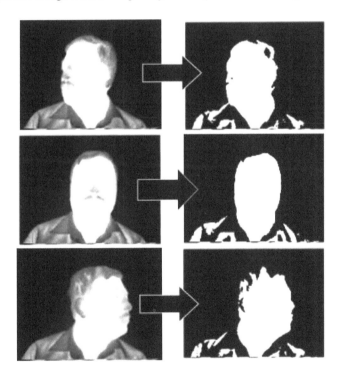

Figure10: Image from the Terravic Facial Infrared Database, before and after binarization.

Figure 11: Multiple exposures of the same person, from different angles, before binarization and LDA, images from the Terravic Facial Infrared Database.

5.1.2. Hard-biometric FWT Experiments

The hard biometric features from the thermal facial images, shown in Figure 11, after binarization were extracted using FWT. Figure 12 shows the wavelet sub-bands. The entire image set is a matrix of size 76800 by 144. This was processed to yield four sub-bands after FWT. The first band, is a matrix of size 9600 by 144, the second a matrix of size 19200 by 144, the third a matrix of size 19200 by 144, and the fourth a matrix of size 38400 by 144. The four sub-bands were merged to form a value matrix, rich in the spatial and frequency components, which served as input to the LDA stage.

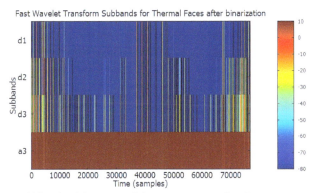

Figure 12: FWT of binarized images, of the same person in Figure 11

5.1.3. Hard-biometric LDA Experiments

LDA was performed on the spatial time-frequency features which formed the confidence matrix of wavelet sub-bands. To further extract points of highest variance. Figure 13 and 14 show a visualization of the time-frequency features, before and after Linear Discriminant Analysis, for the hard biometric features.

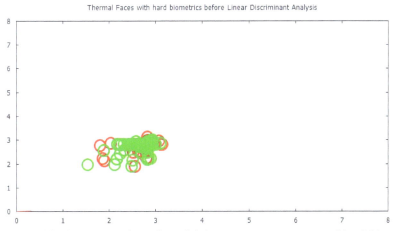

Figure13: Graphical representation of spatial frequency components, of hard biometric features, for thermal faces shown in Figure 10, before LDA

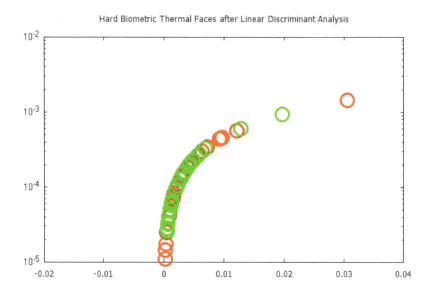

Figure 14: Graphical representation of spatial frequency components, of hard biometric features, for thermal faces shown in Figure 10, after LDA

5.2. Soft-biometrics

This part of the image processing was used for extracting time-frequency and principal components, from each *soft-biometric* attribute. This was achieved by grouping images from the datasets based on the *soft-biometric* attributes presented in Figure 4, Figure 5, Figure 6 and Figure 7.

5.2.1. Soft-biometric FWT Experiments

Figure 15, Figure 16, Figure 17, Figure 18, Figure 19, and Figure 20 show the wavelet sub-bands, for the *soft biometric* attributes after FWT, namely: face wearing glasses, face wearing headgear, face having facial hair, plain face, female face, and male face respectively.

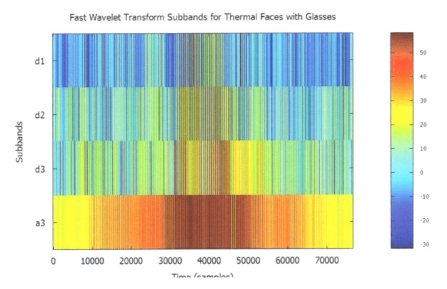

Figure 15: Visualized FWT of face images in glasses, from the Terravic Facial Infrared Database, depicting spatial and frequency information displayed using 4 sub-band

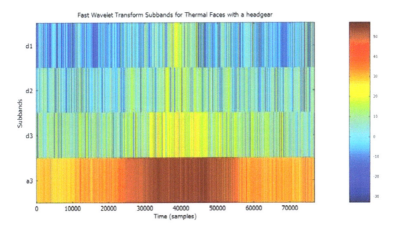

Figure 16: Visualized FWT of face images in headgear, from the Terravic Facial Infrared Database, depicting spatial and frequency information displayed using 4 sub-bands.

31

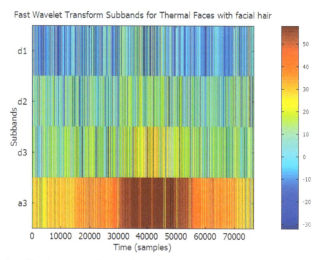

Figure 17: Visualized FWT of face images with facial hair, from the Terravic Facial Infrared Database, depicting spatial and frequency information displayed using 4 sub-bands.

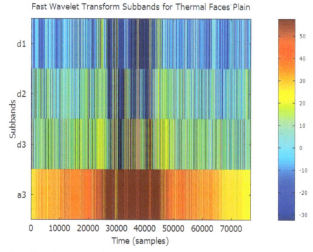

Figure 18: Visualized FWT of plain face images, from the Terravic Facial Infrared Database, depicting spatial and frequency information displayed using 4 sub-bands.

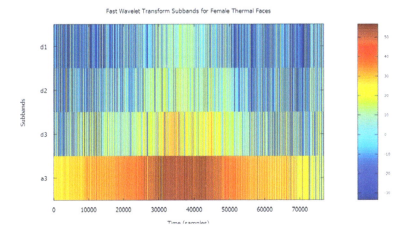

Figure.19: Visualized FWT of female facial images, from the Carl's Infrared Database, depicting time and frequency information displayed using 4 sub-bands.

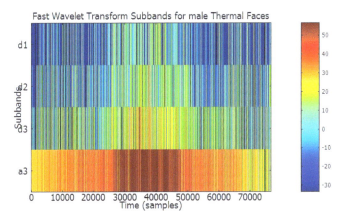

Figure 20: Visualized FWT of male facial images, from the Carl's Infrared Database, depicting time and frequency information displayed using 4 sub-bands.

5.2.2. Soft-biometric LDA experiments

After FWT, LDA was performed on the spatial time-frequency features, to derive points of most variance from the confidence matrix, for each *soft biometric* group. The following figures show a visualization of the spatial frequency features before and after Linear Discriminant Analysis, for face wearing glass, face, face wearing cap, face with hair, plain face, female face, and male face.

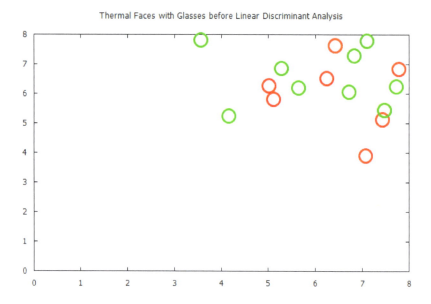

Figure 21: Visualized time-frequency (TF) features, before Linear Discriminant Analysis, for the Terravic Facial Infrared Database images, glass wearing faces

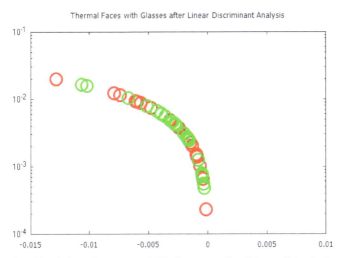

Figure 22: Visualized time-frequency (TF) features after Linear Discriminant Analysis, for images in the Terravic Facial Infrared Database, glass wearing faces

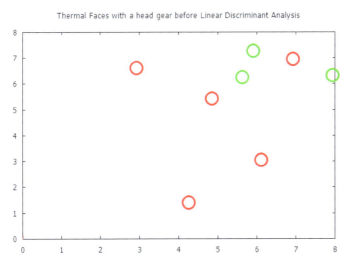

Figure 23. Visualized time-frequency (TF) features, before Linear Discriminant Analysis, for images in the Terravic Facial Infrared Database, cap wearing faces

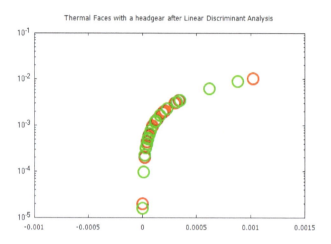

Figure 24: Visualized time-frequency (TF) features after Linear Discriminant Analysis, for the Terravic Facial Infrared Database images, cap wearing faces.

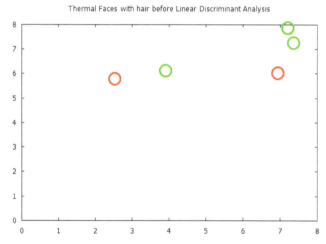

Figure 25: Visualized time-frequency (TF) features, before Linear Discriminant Analysis, for the Terravic Facial Infrared Database images, for faces with facial hair

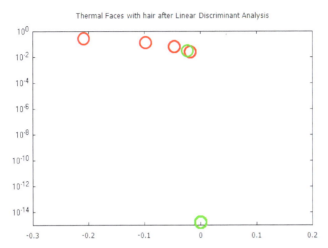

Figure 26: Visualized time-frequency (TF) features, after Linear Discriminant Analysis, for the Terravic Facial Infrared Database images, for faces with facial hair.

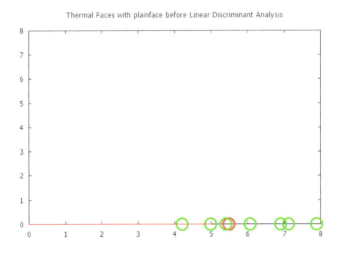

Figure 27: Visualized time-frequency (TF) features, before Linear Discriminant Analysis, for the Terravic Facial Infrared Database images, plain faces

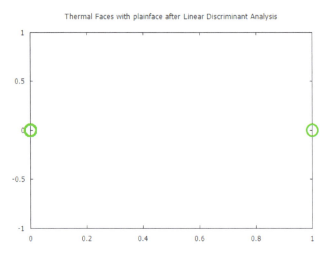

Figure 28: Visualized time-frequency (TF) features, after Linear Discriminant Analysis, for the Terravic Facial Infrared Database images, plain faces

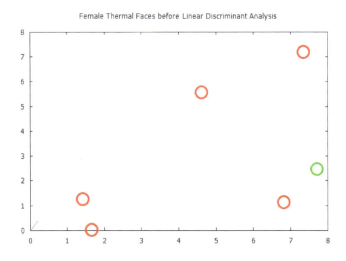

Figure 29: Visualized time-frequency (TF) features, before Linear Discriminant Analysis, for images in the Carl's Infrared Database, female faces.

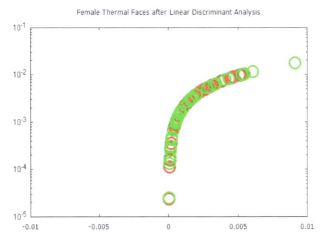

Figure 30: Visualized time-frequency (TF) features, after Linear Discriminant Analysis, for images in the Carl's Infrared Database, male faces.

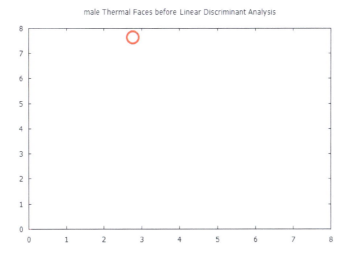

Figure 31: Visualized time-frequency (TF) features, before Linear Discriminant Analysis, for images in the Carl's Infrared Database, male faces

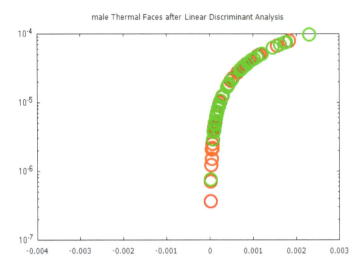

Figure 32: Visualized time-frequency (TF) features, after Linear Discriminant Analysis, for images in the Carl's Infrared Database, male faces

5.3. Summary

The outcome of the feature extraction experiments was stored in a data file using the Matlab format. This was done for both hard biometric and *soft biometric* feature sets. These data files, namely: *Linear Discriminants* for hard biometric features and *Linear Discriminants* for *soft biometric* features. The latter comprising, glass wearing faces, cap wearing face, faces with facial hair, plain faces female faces and male faces. With these the distinguishing features, which describe each of the biometric groups, were known. The objective being to train seven different neural networks, to learn each of the features, and subsequently validate a user's identity using at least two combined. Such that if a user appears, before a thermal sensor, seeking access, without any of the attributes, access would not be granted. But when he or she appears with facial hair, wearing glasses or wearing a cap, access would be granted.

6. *Experiment Two: Deep Learning Neural Networks*

These are a continuation of the pre-processing experiments reported. They were done, using Rasmus Berg Palm's deep learning toolbox, for RBM, DBN, and FFNN.

6.1. Classification

To achieve target vector reconstruction the *Linear Discriminants* realized from the first experiments were used for classification after training. After pre-training the DBN with RBM and further training and classifying with FFNN, a global minimum error was achieved on each training set group. These were: 0.02887 for hard biometric face, 0.038695 for glass wearing face, 0.02381 for headgear wearing face, 0.024629 for facial hair face, 0.0268 for plain face, 0.02369 for female face and 0.03 male face. Also introducing new test images randomly to the algorithm, while matching the FFNN global minimum error with these known values, demonstrated the *soft-biometric* person recognition approach. Making it possible to identify thermal facial images as: face in glasses, hairy face, plain face, face in a headgear. The following traces show the the full batch classification error, from the RBM, DBN, and FFNN algorithms, for each *soft-biometric* group.

6.2. Plots

The plots from each training session, for RBM, DBN, and FFNN, are graphically shown below for each of the seven semantic categories. In the following order: hard biometric face, faces wearing glasses, faces wearing a cap, faces having facial hair, faces plain, female faces, and male faces. Each one shows an improvement, in the algorithm's training error, up until the FFNN session. At which point the algorithm, fully learns the data and makes predictions on it, with little error.

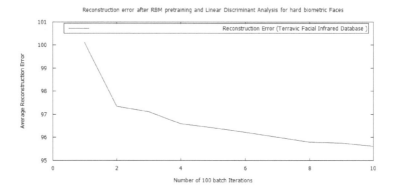

Figure 33: RBM classification error after LDA feature extraction applying the time-frequency features of images from the Terravic Facial Infrared Database, facial hard biometrics user.

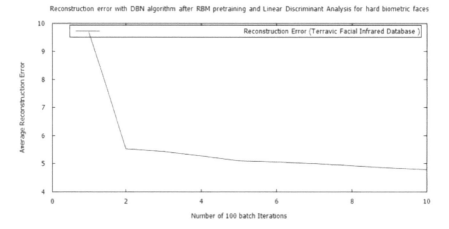

Figure 34: DBN classification error, after RBM pre-training for Terravic Facial Infrared Database images, user facial hard biometrics.

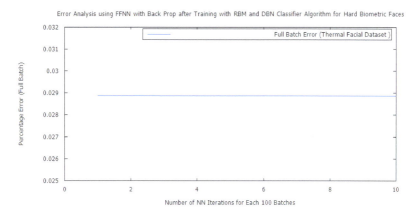

Figure 35: FFNN classification full batch error after DBN target vector reconstruction applying RBM pre-training and LDA feature extraction using the time-frequency features of Terravic Facial Infrared Database images, user facial hard biometric.

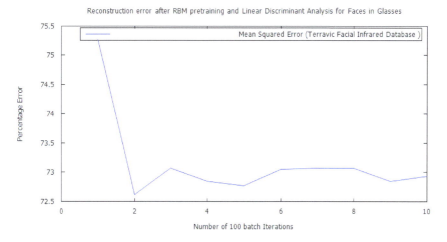

Figure 36: RBM classification error after LDA feature extraction applying the time-frequency features of Terravic Facial Infrared Database images, faces in glasses.

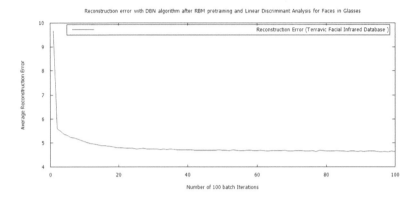

Figure 37: DBN classification error, after RBM pre-training for Terravic Facial Infrared Database images, glass wearing faces.

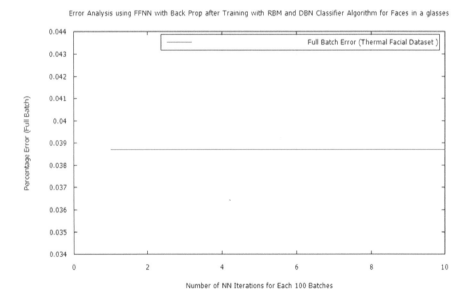

Figure 38: FFNN classification error after DBN target vector reconstruction with RBM pre-training and LDA feature extraction applying the time-frequency features of Terravic Facial Infrared Database images, glass wearing face group.

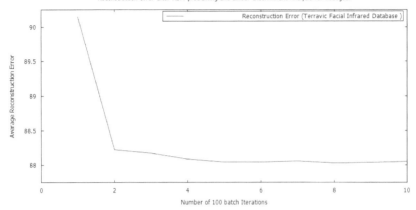

Figure 39: RBM classification error after LDA feature extraction applying the time-frequency features of Terravic Facial Infrared Database images, headgear faces.

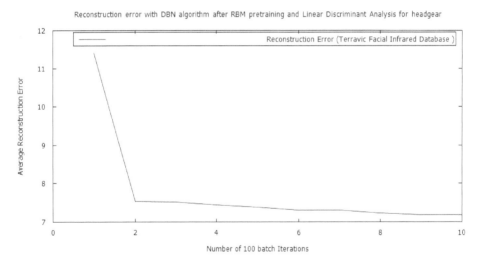

Figure 40: DBN classification error, after RBM pre-training for Terravic Facial Infrared Database images, headgear wearing faces.

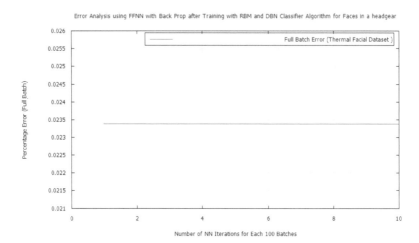

Figure 41:FFNN classification error after DBN target vector reconstruction with RBM pre-training and LDA feature extraction applying the time-frequency features of Terravic Facial Infrared Database images, headgear wearing group.

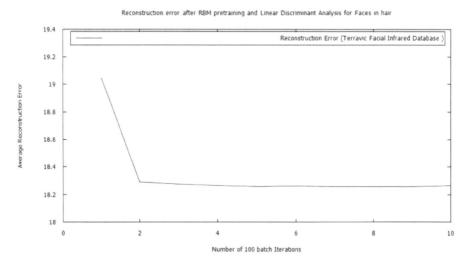

Figure 42: DBN classification error, after RBM pre-training for Terravic Facial Infrared Database images, faces having facial hair.

46

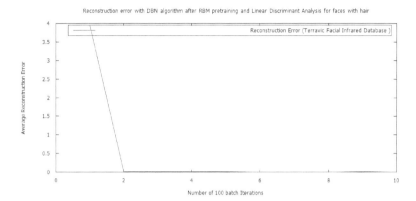

Figure 43: DBN classification error, after RBM pre-training for Terravic Facial Infrared Database images, faces having facial hair.

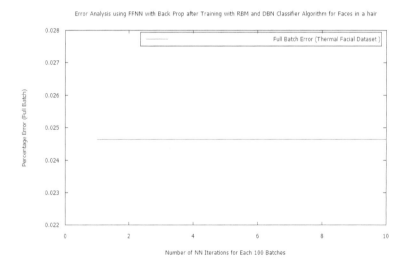

Figure 44: FFNN classification error after DBN target vector reconstruction with RBM pre-training and LDA feature extraction applying the time-frequency(TF) features of Terravic Facial Infrared Database images, hairy faces group.

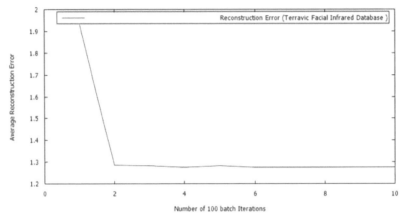

Figure 45: DBN classification error, after RBM pre-training for Terravic Facial Infrared Database images, plain faces.

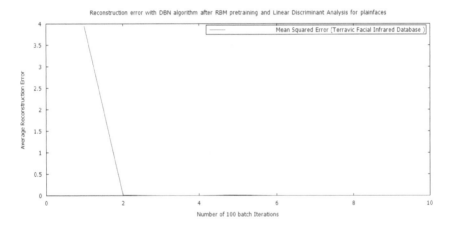

Figure 46: DBN classification error, after RBM pre-training for Terravic Facial Infrared Database images, plain faces.

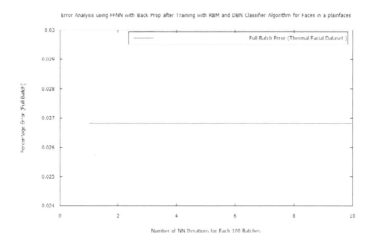

Figure 47: FFNN classification error after DBN target vector reconstruction with RBM pre-training and LDA feature extraction applying the time-frequency features of Terravic Facial Infrared Database images, plain face group.

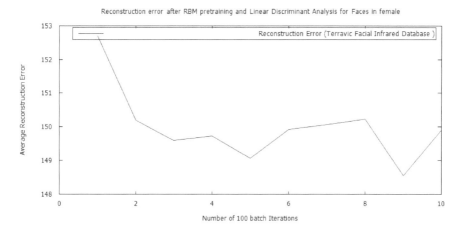

Figure 48: RBM classification error after LDA feature extraction applying the time-frequency features of Terravic Facial Infrared Database images, female faces.

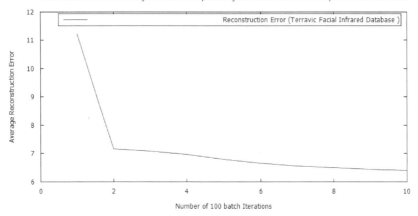

Figure 49: DBN classification error, after RBM pre-training for Terravic Facial Infrared Database images, female faces.

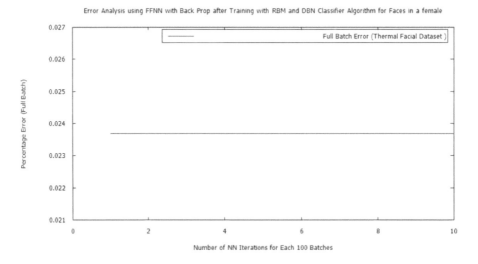

Figure 50: FFNN classification error after DBN target vector reconstruction with RBM pre-training and LDA feature extraction applying the time-frequency features of Terravic Facial Infrared Database images, female face.

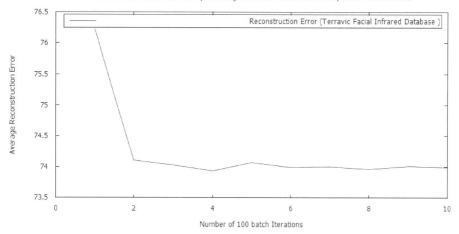

Figure 51: RBM classification error after LDA feature extraction applying the time-frequency features of Terravic Facial Infrared Database images, male faces.

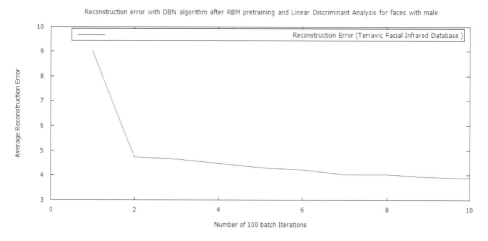

Figure 52: DBN classification error, after RBM pre-training for Terravic Facial Infrared Database images, male faces.

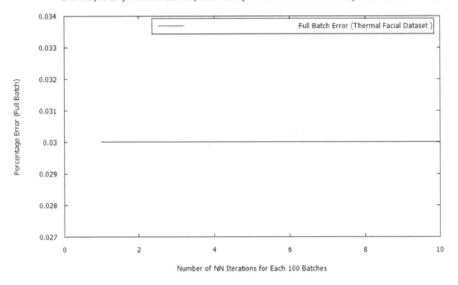

Error Analysis using FFNN with Back Prop after Training with RBM and DBN Classifier Algorithm for Faces in a male

Figure 53: FFNN classification error after DBN target vector reconstruction with RBM pre-training and LDA feature extraction applying the time-frequency features of Terravic Facial Infrared Database images, male face.

6.3. Result analysis

Table 3: RBM Test Error Results Per Semantics Attribute Group

Semantic Attribute	RBM error
hard biometric face	95.609
Faces in glasses	72.93
Faces wearing a cap/headgear	88.051
Faces with facial hair	18.265
Faces with a plain face	1.2756
Female faces	147.9
Male faces	73.98

Table 4: Test Error Results Per Semantic Attribute Group

Semantic Attribute	DBN error
hard biometric face	4.7895
Faces in glasses	4.6364
Faces wearing a cap/headgear	7.182
Faces with facial hair	0.026
Faces with a plain face	0.026
Female faces	6.406
Male faces	3.926

Table 5: Test Error Results Per Semantic Attribute Group

Semantic Attribute	FFNN error
hard biometric face	0.02887
Faces in glasses	0.038695
Faces wearing a cap/headgear	0.02381
Faces with facial hair	0.02462
Faces with a plain face	0.0268
Female faces	0.02369
Male faces	0.03

Applying the RBM pre-trained DBN, with FFNN classifier algorithm method, to the *Linear Discriminants* from the thermal facial images, it was observed that:

- Time-frequency (TF) components, gleaned from Fast Wavelet Transform, aided LDA in the facial thermal image investigation.
- On each of the biometric training sets a low reconstruction error was achieved, using DBN after pre-training with RBM, through target vector reconstruction. This excepted faces wearing glasses, which needed to be trained using a bigger batch size of 100 to achieve a test error of 4.6364%. This value was further reduced to 0.038695% after additional training with the FFNN algorithm.
- The other biometric groups didn't require additional training and were trained using a batch size of 10.
- With the use of back propagation, DBN pre-trained with RBM algorithm successfully learned the features of the *soft-biometric* training sets. This was possible without lengthy training sessions.

- As in the case of glass wearing face including feature learning, and training with FFNN, aided the further reduction of the classification error.
- The reduced classification error realized, by applying FFNN with DBN pre-trained using RBM and LDA, showed that the algorithm would recognize each *soft biometric* trait and differentiate one from the other.

6.4. Observations

Classifying using FWT, LDA and RBM pre-trained DBN with FFNN algorithms, yielded less error of 0.038695% on the glass wearing semantic group. This was for the following reasons:

- The DBN classifier runs faster and uses fewer system resources because of the structure of its RBM unit. Thus it learns more about the problem within a short period.
- The DBN classifier uses back propagation during training for error reconstruction.
- The DBN classifier, is ensembled with a Feed-Forward Neural Network (FFNN) which further, learns the problem and reduces the classification errors.

Using images in the Terravic Facial Infrared and Carl's databases *Multi-biometric* person recognition in thermal images is demonstrated. This was done using FFNN classifiers, after feature extraction with FWT and LDA, and RBM pre-trained DBN for feature learning. *Hard biometric* features, coupled with outward attributes, such as face wearing glass, face wearing cap, face with facial hair, plain face, female face, and male face, of persons in the datasets, were learned for multi-biometric grouping. Trial images not in the training sets were afterwards recognized multi-biometrically, with both their hard biometric traits coupled with any of the six *soft biometric* traits, using the technique. Table 6 shows a tabulation of the experiment results.

Table 6: FWT, LDA, RBM, DBN, and FFNN Multi-Biometric Experiment Results Per Semantic Attribute Group

Experiment	Result
Feature Extraction FWT	Numbers
FWT Sub-band one	9600 features
FWT Sub-band two	9600 features
FWT Sub-band three	19200 features
FWT Sub-band four	38400 features
FWT Sub-band four + LDA+RBM Hard-biometric features	4.7895 %
FWT Sub-band four + LDA+RBM Glass faces	4.6364%
FWT Sub-band four + LDA+RBM Head gear faces	0.026 %
FWT Sub-band four + LDA+RBM Facial hair faces	0.026 %
FWT Sub-band four + LDA+RBM Plain faces	0.026 %
FWT Sub-band four + LDA+RBM Female faces	6.406 %
FWT Sub-band four + LDA+RBM Male faces	3.926 %
FWT Sub-band four + LDA+RBM+DBN+FFNN Hard-biometric features	0.02887
FWT Sub-band four + LDA+RBM+DBN+FFNN glass wearing faces	0.038695 %
FWT Sub-band four + LDA+RBM+DBN+FFNN head gear wearing faces	0.02381 %
FWT Sub-band four + LDA+RBM+DBN+FFNN faces with facial hair	0.024629 %
FWT Sub-band four + LDA+RBM+DBN+FFNN plain faces	0.0268 %
FWT Sub-band four + LDA+RBM+DBN+FFNN Female faces	0.02369 %
FWT Sub-band four + LDA+RBM+DBN+FFNN Male faces	1.3 %

6.5. Summary

The outcome, of the feature classification experiments are stored in a data file using the Matlab format. This is done for both, hard biometric and soft biometric, feature sets. These data files contain the error on the test set, for the prediction of the unknown variable (y) given the known variable (X) after training, for the hard biometric and *soft biometric* features. The latter comprising, faces wearing glass, faces wearing cap, face having facial hair, plain face, female face, and male faces. With these the extent to which the neural network knows each of the biometric, features are noted. Based on the low classification error on each of the test sets, as shown in Table 6, the system can recognize biometric features not in the training set, such as:

- Facial, hard biometric, features of the user used in training the algorithm, as shown in Figure 10.
- Faces of a user when in glasses, as shown in Figure 4.
- Faces of a user when wearing a cap, as shown in Figure 5.
- Faces of a user when having facial hair, as shown in Figure 6.
- Faces of a user when plain without facial hair, as shown in Figure 7.
- The face of a female user.
- The face of a male user.

With these biometric traits additional layers of security can be introduced into a person recognition system. Asides using a user's facial hard biometric features for authentication, two, three, four or five other biometric attributes can be used to make a system more difficult to fool. As a result of such complexity, a forger would find it hard to guess what traits the system would need for recognition to take place. Table 7 shows fifteen possible multi-biometric feature configurations, based on the traits used in this research, along with their security levels. Each combination can work, using all traits or only one, before a person's identity is confirmed. In either mode, if a user appears before the sensor without at least one requisite *soft biometric* trait based on system requirements, the user's identity would not be verified.

The advantage of the system being that it can acquire all the needed biometric traits using a single sensor. Thus a hacker who watches while a user's identity is being verified, using this method, would be unable to know exactly what biometric attribute to forge.

Table 7: Multi Biometric Feature Configurations and Security Levels

	Biometric Features	Security Level
1	Countenance + Glasses	Robust
2	Countenance + Cap	Robust
3	Countenance + Facial hair	Robust
4	Countenance + Plain face	Robust
5	Countenance + Gender	Robust
6	Countenance + Glasses + Cap	More Robust
7	Countenance + Glasses + Facial hair	More Robust
8	Countenance + Glasses + Plain face	More Robust
9	Countenance + Glasses + Gender	More Robust
10	Countenance + Glasses + Cap + Facial hair	Much More Robust
11	Countenance + Glasses + Cap + Plain face	Much More Robust
12	Countenance + Glasses + Cap + Gender	Much More Robust
13	Countenance + Glasses + Facial hair + Gender	Much More Robust
14	Countenance + Glasses + Cap + Facial hair + Gender	Most Robust
15	Countenance + Glasses + Cap + Plain face + Gender	Most Robust

7. Experiment Three: Multi biometric person recognition

Using the trained algorithm cluster, with test results tabulated in Table 12. The system was tested in *verification mode* with the person in Figure 10 as a user. Working with a multi-biometric combinations of traits: Countenance + Glasses + Facial hair + Gender. Which are the user's hard-biometric features, glass wearing features, facial hair features and gender traits. The hard-biometric trait is taken as X (features to be learned) while the facial hair trait as the base for comparison y (unknown feature to be predicted y). Tests are done to confirm the other three soft-biometric characteristics and verify his identity.

7.1. Tests1 hard-biometric and facial hair algorithms

The first test is conducted to verify the hard-biometric features of the user for the presence of facial hair. By using the X variables after LDA, of the hard-biometric features, and the y variables after LDA, of the facial hair features. The RBM, DBN and

FFNN tests were conducted to verify, that the user with the hard-biometric features (presented to the sensor), has facial hair as the authentic user. The FFNN result is shown, in comparison with those from the training test, in Table 8.

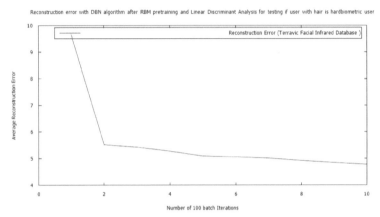

Figure 54: Error for facial hair algorithm testing hard biometric features for the presence of facial hair using RBM, LDA, and FWT for images from the Terravic Facial Infrared Database

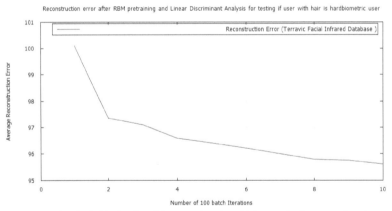

Figure 55: Error for facial hair algorithm testing hard biometric features for the presence of facial hair using RBM, LDA, and FWT for images from the Terravic Facial Infrared Database

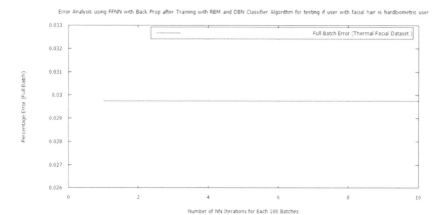

Figure 56: Error for facial hair algorithm testing if the hard biometric user is a user with facial hair using FFNN, DBN, RBM, LDA, and FWT for images from the Terravic Facial Infrared Database.

Table 8: FFNN Check for Facial Hair and Hard Biometric Traits

	Semantic Attribute	**FFNN error**
Training test	Hard-biometric face	0.02887
Training test	Faces with facial hair	0.02462
Verification test	Check if the user with hard-biometric features has facial hair as the main user does.	0.02975

7.2. Tests2 glass wearing and facial hair algorithms

The second test is conducted to verify that the user with facial hair, whose hard-biometric features have been confirmed, is putting on glasses. By using the X variables after LDA, of the glass wearing features for the user to be verified, and the y variables after LDA, of facial hair features. Based on facial hair attributes, the RBM, DBN, and FFNN tests were conducted to verify that the user wearing glasses (presented to the sensor) is the authentic user. The FFNN result is shown, in comparison with those from the training test, in Table 9 below.

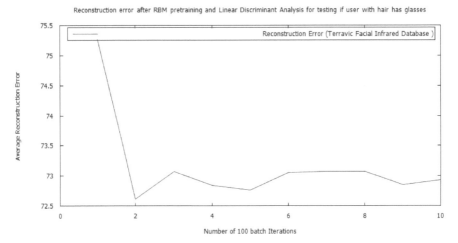

Figure 57: Error for facial hair algorithm testing glass wearing face for the presence of facial hair using RBM, LDA, and FWT for images from the Terravic Facial Infrared Database.

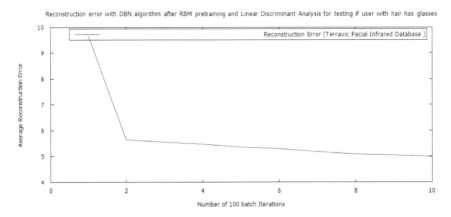

Figure 58: Error for facial hair algorithm testing glass wearing face for the presence of facial hair using DBN, RBM, LDA, and FWT for images from the Terravic Facial Infrared Database.

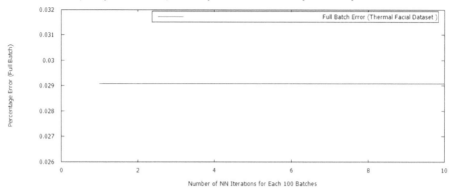

Figure 59: Error for facial hair algorithm testing glass wearing face for the presence of facial hair using FFNN, DBN, RBM, LDA, and FWT for images from the Terravic Facial Infrared Database

Table 9: FFNN Check for Facial Hair and Glass Wearing Face Traits

	Semantic Attribute	**FFNN error**
Training test	Faces with facial hair	0.02462
Training test	Faces in glasses	0.038695
Verification Test	Check if the user with facial hair has glasses	0.02908

7.3. Test 3, male gender and facial hair algorithms

The third test is conducted to verify that the user, with facial hair whose hard-biometric and glass wearing features have been confirmed, is masculine. By using the X variables after LDA, of the male gender features (from the sensor) of the user to be verified, and the Y variables after LDA of the facial hair features. RBM, DBN and FFNN tests are conducted to verify that the male, presented to the sensor, is the authentic user. The FFNN result is shown, in comparison with those from the training test, in Table 10.

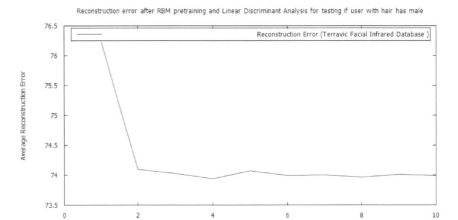

Figure 60: Error for facial hair algorithm testing male faces for the presence of facial hair using RBM, LDA, and FWT for images from the Terravic Facial Infrared Database

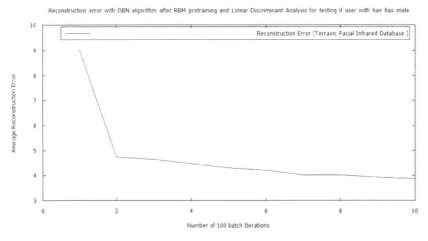

Figure 61: Error for facial hair algorithm testing male face for the presence of facial hair using DBN, RBM, LDA, and FWT for images from the Terravic Facial Infrared Database

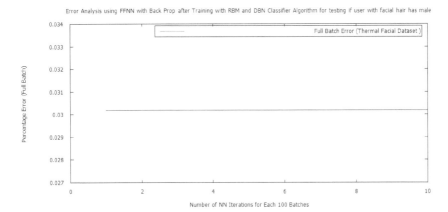

Figure 62: Error for male gender algorithm testing facial hair face for male gender using FFNN, DBN, RBM, LDA, and FWT for images from the Terravic Facial Infrared Database

Table 10: FFNN Check for Facial Hair and Male Gender Soft-Biometric Traits

	Semantic Attribute	**FFNN error**
Training test	Faces with facial hair	0.02462
Training test	Male faces	0.03
Verification Test	Check if a user with facial hair is male	0.03018

To ascertain that the person requesting verification is the authentic person. The results are summarized below.

7.4. Explanation

By comparing the FFNN error, from each of the cross-feature tests, to those from the algorithm. The trait check is seen to pass for each characteristic, based on comparison to the algorithm's test results. This is explained for each test as shown below.

7.4.1. Tests1, hard-biometric and facial hair algorithms

The similarity of the FFNN verification test results to those of the hard-biometric features, from the training test, show that they belong to the original user. This also shows that the hard-biometric trait, used in training the algorithm, has a close similarity to those possessed by the user being verified.

7.4.2. Tests2, glass wearing, and facial hair algorithms

The similarity of the FFNN verification test results to those of the face in glasses biometric features, from the training test, show that they belong to the original user. Since they have a value that is between that outputted by the glass algorithm and the one belonging to facial hair, as these two *soft-biometric* traits are present, in the X and y test data. Showing that the biometric trait, used in training the algorithm, has a close similarity to those possessed by the user being verified.

7.4.3. Test 3, male gender and facial hair algorithms

The similarity of the FFNN verification test result to those of the male gender biometric features, from the training test, show that they belong to the original user. Since they have a value that is closer to that of the male gender algorithm than the one belonging to facial hair. This also shows that the male gender biometric trait, used in training the algorithm, has a close similarity to those possessed by the user being verified.

7.4.4. Summary

From the tests, the first assumption was that the person being verified has facial hair and this was used to verify the other three traits, one after the other. The approach adds redundancy into the system with each trait used, to verify the other, one after the other. Such that if facial hair is absent, glasses would be and if glasses and facial hair are absent, the masculine features would be. Thus increasing robustness and system performance. In *identification mode*, for a large population size of millions, the technique can help to achieve high distinctiveness, high persistence, better performance, high acceptability and low potential for spoofing.

8. Conclusion

Multi-biometric person recognition, using thermal images to improve biometric security, is established, with images from Carl's database and the Terravic Facial Infrared Database. This was done using FWT, LDA and RBM pre-trained DBN with FFNN classifiers. The hard biometric attribute, of shape of head, was combined with outward attributes, such as face in glasses, face in a cap/head gear, face with facial hairs, plain face, female face and male face, using persons in the thermal facial datasets. These were learned, used for multi-biometric classification and then multi-biometric person recognition. Using the parallel mode of operation, through score fusion, a test user possessing these traits was verified with the technique. Showing how biometric system security can be fortified through a combination of hard and soft-biometric traits.

Conflict of Interest

The authors declare no conflict of interest.

Acknowledgment

The financial assistance of the National Research Foundation (NRF) towards this research is hereby acknowledged. Opinions expressed and conclusions arrived at, are those of the author and are not necessarily to be attributed to the NRF.

References

[1] Moreno-Moreno, M., Fierrez, J., and Ortega-Garcia, J., "Millimeter- and Submillimeter-Wave Imaging Technologies for Biometric Purposes," in Proceedings of XXIV Simposium Nacional de Union Cientica Internacional de Radio, URSI, Spain, September 2009.

[2] D.L. Narayanan, R.N. Saladi, J.L. Fox, "Ultraviolet radiation and skin cancer," Int. J. Dermatol., vol. 49, no. 9, pp. 978–986, Sep. 2010.

[3] Moreno-Moreno, M., Fierrez, J., and Ortega-Garcia, J., "Biometrics Beyond the Visible Spectrum: Imaging Technologies and Applications," in Proceedings of BioID-Multicomm, LNCS 5707, 154–161, Springer, September 2009.

[4] E. Hurwitz, A. N. Hasan, and C. Orji, "Soft biometric thermal face recognition using FWT and LDA feature extraction method with RBM DBN and FFNN classifier algorithms," ICIIP, 2017, pp. 1 – 6, doi: 10.1109/ICIIP.2017.8313796.

[5] A.Meraoumia, S.Chitroub, A. Bouridane "Multimodal Biometric Person Recognition System based on Fingerprint & Finger-Knuckle-Print Using Correlation Filter Classifier", Communications (ICC), 2012 IEEE International Conference, Ottawa, Canada pages 820 - 824.

[6] Galbally, J., Marcel, S., & Fierrez, J. (2014). Biometric Antispoofing Methods: A Survey in Face Recognition. IEEE Access, 2, 1530-1552

[7] X. Geng, L. Wang, M. Li, Q. Wu, and K. Smith-Miles. Adaptive fusion of gait and face for human identification in video. In Applications of Computer Vision, 2008. WACV 2008. IEEE Workshop on, pages 1-6, Jan. 2008.

[8] L.Hong, A.k.Jain, S. Pankanti, "Can multibiometrics improve performance ?", Proc. AutoID'99, pp. 59-64, 1999-Oct

[9] IEEE OTCBVS WS Series Bench; Roland Miezianko, Terravic Research Infrared Database.

[10] V. Espinosa-Dur ́o, M. Faundez-Zanuy, and J. Mekyska, "A new face database simultaneously acquired in visible, near-infrared and thermal spectrums," Cognitive Computation, vol. 5, no. 1, pp. 119–135, 2013

[11] A. K. Jain, P. J. Flynn, and A. Ross. Handbook of Biometrics. Springer, 2007.

[12] H.T.F. Rhodes. Alphonse Bertillon: Father of scientific detection. Pattern Recognition Letters, 1956.

[13] L. Wen and G-D. Guo. A computational approach to body mass index prediction from face images. Image and Vision Computing, 31(5):392–400, 2013.

[14] R. Zewail, A. Elsafi, M. Saeb, and N. Hamdy. Soft and hard biometrics fusion for improved identity verification. In Proc. of IEEE International Midwest Symposium on Circuits and Systems, volume 1, pages I – 225–8, 2004.

[15] D. Reid and M. Nixon. Imputing human descriptions in semantic biometrics. In Proc. of ACM Workshop on Multimedia in Forensics, Security and Intelligence, 2010.

[16] A. K. Jain, A. Ross, and S. Prabhakar, "An introduction to biometric recognition," IEEE Trans. Circuits Syst. Video Technology, Special Issue Image- and Video-Based Biomet., vol. 14, no. 1, pp. 4–20, Jan. 2004.

[17] R.M. Bolle, S. Pankanti, and N.K. Ratha, "Evaluation Techniques for Biometrics-Based Authentication Systems (FRR)," Proc. 15th Int'l Conf. Pattern Recognition, vol. 2, pp. 831-837, Sept. 2000.

[18] N. Kumar, A. C. Berg, P. N. Belhumeur, and S. K. Nayar. Attribute and simile classifiers for face verification. In Proc. of International Conference on Computer Vision, 2009.

[19] S. Z. Li and A. K. Jain, Eds., Handbook of Face Recognition. New York: Springer Verlag, 2004.

[20] D. Reid and M. Nixon. Using comparative human descriptions for soft biometrics. In Proc. of International Joint Conference on Biometrics, 2011.

[21] S. Samangooei, B. Guo, and Mark S. Nixon. The use of semantic human description as a soft biometric. In Proc. of IEEE International Conference on Biometrics: Theory, Applications and Systems, 2008.

[22] A.K. Jain, S.C. Dass, and K. Nandakumar. *Soft biometric* traits for personal recognition systems. In Proceedings of ICBA, pages 1–40. Springer, 2004.

[23] A. Dantcheva, C. Velardo, A. D'Angelo, and J.-L. Dugelay. Bag of *soft biometrics* for person identification. New trends and challenges. Multimedia Tools and Applications, 51:739–777, 2011.

[24] D. Bhattacharjee, A. Seal, S. Ganguly, M. Nasipuri, and D.K. Basu, "A Comparative Study of Human Thermal Face Recognition Based on Haar Wavelet Transform and Local Binary Pattern," Computational Intelligence and Neuroscience, vol. 2012, Article ID 261089, 12 pages, 2012. oi:10.1155/2012/261089

[25] L. Hong, A. K. Jain, S. Pankanti, "Can multibiometrics improve performance ?", Proc. AutoID'99, pp. 59-64, 1999-Oct

[26] B. Martinez, X. Binefa, and M. Pantic. Facial component detection in thermal imagery. In Proc. IEEE Conference on Computer Vision and Pattern Recognition Workshops, pages 48–54, 2010

[27] C. Herrmann, T. Müller, D. Willersinn, J. Beyerer, "Real-time person detection in low-resolution thermal infrared imagery with MSER and CNNs", in Proc. Electro-Optical and Infrared Systems, SPIE, 2016

[28] A. Krizhevsky, I. Sutskever and G. Hinton. ImageNet Classification with Deep Convolutional Neural Networks. In Advances in Neural information Processing Systems 25, pages 1106-1114, 2012

[29] W. Shangfei, L. Zhilei, L. Siliang, L. Yanpeng, W. Guobing, P. Peng, C. Fei and W. Xufa, "A Natural Visible and Infrared Facial Expression Database for Expression Recognition and Emotion Inference", IEEE Transactions on Multimedia, vol.12, no.7, pp.682-691, Nov. 2010

[30] K. Tai, S. Blain, and T. Chau, "A review of emerging access technologies for individuals with severe motor impairments," Assist. Technol., vol. 20, pp. 204–219, 2008

[31] Bhowmik, M.K., Saha, K., Majumder, S., Majumder, G., Saha, A., Sarma, A.N., Bhattacharjee, D., Basu, D.K., Nasipuri, M., Corcoran, Peter M. 'Thermal infrared face recognition – a biometric identification technique for robust security system'. Reviews, Refinements and New Ideas in Face Recognition. 2011, 07, Zieglergase, Vienna, Austria, Europe: InTech Open Access Publisher, Vienna Office, ISBN: 978-953-307-368-2, (open access publisher of scientific books and journals)

[32] A. Seal, S. Ganguly, D. Bhattacharjee, M. Nasipuri, D. K. Basu, "Minutiae Based Thermal Human Face Recognition using Label Connected Component Algorithm," Procedia Technology, In 2nd International Conference on Computer, Communication, Control and Information Technology (C3IT-2012), February 25 - 26, 2012. multilayer perceptron

[33] S. Cho, L. Wang, and W. J. Ong. Thermal imprint feature analysis for face recognition. ISIE, pages 1875–1880, 2009.

[34] O. Arandjelovic′c, R. Hammoud, and R. Cipolla. On person authentication by fusing visual and thermal face biometrics. In Proc. IEEE Conference on Advanced Video and Singal Based Surveillance, pages 50–56, 2006.

[35] M. Piccardi, "Background subtraction techniques: a review," in Proc. of the IEEE International Conference on Systems, Man and Cybernet- ics (SMC), vol. 4, pp. 3099-3104, IEEE, Oct. 2004.

[36] S. Se and M. Brady, "Ground plane estimation, error analysis and applications," Robotics and Autonomous Systems, vol. 39, no. 2, pp. 59-71, 2002.

[37] K. C. Sofiane Yous, Hamid Laga, "People detection and tracking with world-z map from a single stereo camera," in Proc. of the International Workshop on Visual Surveillance (VS) - (ECCV), (Marseille, France), October 2008.

[38] A. Broggi, M. Bertozzi, A. Fascioli, and M. Sechi, "Shape-based pedes-trian detection," in Proc. of the IEEE Intelligent Vehicles Symposium(IV), pp. 215-220, 2000.

[39] D. Vaquero, R. Feris, D. Tran, L. Brown, A. Hampapur, and M. Turk. Attribute-based people search in surveillance environments. In Proc. of IEEE Workshop on Applications of Computer Vision, 2009.

[40] B. Wu and R. Nevatia, "Detection of multiple, partially occluded humans in a single image by bayesian combination of edgelet part de-tectors," in Proc. of the International Conference on Computer Vi-sion(ICCV), 2005.

[41] G. Beylkin, R. Coifman, and V. Rokhlin. Fast wavelet transforms and numerical algorithms I. Communications on Pure and Applied Mathematics, 44 (2):141–183, March 1991

[42] M. Jones, P. Viola, P. Viola, M. J. Jones, D. Snow, and D. Snow, "De-tecting pedestrians using patterns of motion and appearance," in Proc. of the International Conference on Computer Vision(ICCV), pp. 734-741, 2003.

[43] Q. Zhu, M.-C. Yeh, K.-T. Cheng, and S. Avidan, "Fast human de-tection using a cascade of histograms of oriented gradients," in Proc. of the IEEE Conference on Computer Vision and Pattern Recogni-tion(CVPR), (Washington, DC, USA), pp. 1491-1498, IEEE Computer Society, 2006.

[44] A. Mohan, C. Papageorgiou, and T. Poggio, "Example based object detection in images by components," IEEE Transactions on Pattern Analysis and Machine Intelligence (PAMI), vol. 23, pp. 349-361, 2001.

[45] B. Wu and R. Nevatia, "Detection and tracking of multiple, partially occluded humans by bayesian combination of edgelet based part de-tectors," International Journal of Computer Vision(IJCV), vol. 75, pp. 247-266, Nov. 2007

[46] L.Trujillo, G. Olague, R.Hammoud and B. Hernandez. Automatic Feature Localization in Thermal Images for Facial Expression Recognition. Computer Vision and Pattern Recognition-Workshops, IEEE Computer Society Conference, p. 14, 2005.

[47] Martinez B, Binefa X, Pantic M. Facial Component Detection in Thermal Imagery. Computer Vision and Pattern Recognition Workshops (CVPRW), IEEE Computer Society Conference, p. 48-54, 2010.

[48] F.Q Al-Khalidi, R. Saatchi, D. Burke, H. Elphick. Tracking human face features in thermal images for respiration monitoring. Int Conf Computer Systems and Applications(AICCSA), p. 1-6, 2010.

[49] S. Prabhakar, S. Pankanti, and A. K. Jain, "Biometric recognition: Security and privacy concerns," IEEE Security Privacy Mag., vol. 1, no. 2, pp. 33–42, 2003

[50] R.M. Bolle, S. Pankanti, and N.K. Ratha, "Evaluation Techniques for Biometrics-Based Authentication Systems (FRR)," Proc. 15th Int'l Conf. Pattern Recognition, vol. 2, pp. 831-837, Sept. 2000.

[51] Joshua C. Klontz and Anil K. Jain. A case study on unconstrained facial recognition using the boston marathon bombings suspects. Technical Report, (MSU-CSE-13-4), 2013

[52] S. Z. Li and A. K. Jain, Eds., Handbook of Face Recognition. New York: Springer Verlag, 2004.

[53] International Biometric Group, "Independent Testing of Iris RecognitionTechnology May 2005 [Online]. Available: http://www.biometricgroup. com/reports/public/reports/ITIRT_report.htm.

[54] A.K. Jain, S. C. Dass, and K. Nandakumar. Can *soft biometric* traits assist user recognition? In Proceedings of SPIE, volume 5404, pages 561–572, 2004

[55] W. J. Scheirer, N. Kumar, K. Ricanek, P. N. Belhumeur, and T. E. Boult. Fusing with context: a Bayesian approach to combining descriptive attributes. In Proc. of International Joint Conference on Biometrics, 2011

[56] S. Denman, C. Fookes, A. Bialkowski, and S. Sridharan. Softbiometrics: Unconstrained authentication in a surveillance environment. In Proc. of International Conference on Digital Image Computing: Techniques and Applications, pages 196–203, 2009

[57] N. Holighaus, Z. Pr'u'sa, C. Wiesmeyr, "Designing tight filter bank frames for nonlinear frequency scales, sampling Theory and Applications," 2015. [online]. Available: http://ltfat.github.io/notes/ltfatnote039.pdf.

[58] P. Wagner, "Bytefish face recognition algorithms for MATLAB/GNU Octave and Python," 2015. [Online]. Available: https://github.com/bytefish/facerec.

[59] R. B. Palm, "Prediction as a candidate for learning deep hierarchical models of data," 2012. [Online]. Available: http://www2.imm.dtu.dk/pubdb/views/publication_details.php?id=6284

[60] G. Beylkin, R. Coifman, and V. Rokhlin. Fast wavelet transforms and numerical algorithms I. Communications on Pure and Applied Mathematics, 44(2):141–183, March 1991.

[61] L. Sirovitch and M. Kirby, "Low-Dimensional Procedure for the Characterization of Human Faces," J. Optical Soc. of Am. A, vol. 2, pp. 519-524, 1987.

[62] P.L. Søndergaard, B. Torrésani, P.Balazs. The Linear Time-Frequency Analysis Toolbox. International Journal of Wavelets, Multiresolution Analysis and Information Processing, 10(4), 2012.

[63] M. Turk and A. Pentland, "Eigenfaces for Recognition," J. Cognitive Neuroscience, vol. 3, no. 1, 1991.

[64] R.A. Fisher, "The Use of Multiple Measures in Taxonomic Problems," Ann. Eugenics, vol. 7, pp. 179-188, 1936.

[65] V. Nair and G. E. Hinton. Rectified linear units improve restricted boltzmann machines. In Proc. 27th International Conference on Machine Learning, 2010.

[66] G. E. Hinton, S. Osindero, and Y. Teh, "A fast learning algorithm for deep belief nets," Neural computation, vol. 18, no. 7, pp. 1527–1554, 2006.

[67] A. K. Jain, A. Ross, and S. Pankanti, "Biometrics: a tool for information security," IEEE Transactions on Information Forensics and Security, vol. 1, no. 2, pp. 125–143, 2006.

Publisher: Eliva Press SRL

Email: info@elivapress.com

Eliva Press is an independent publishing house established for the publication and dissemination of academic works all over the world. Company provides high quality and professional service for all of our authors.

Our Services:
Free of charge, open-minded, eco-friendly, innovational.

-Free standard publishing services (manuscript review, step-by-step book preparation, publication, distribution, and marketing).
-No financial risk. The author is not obliged to pay any hidden fees for publication.
-Editors. Dedicated editors will assist step by step through the projects.
-Money paid to the author for every book sold. Up to 50% royalties guaranteed.
-ISBN (International Standard Book Number). We assign a unique ISBN to every Eliva Press book.
-Digital archive storage. Books will be available online for a long time. We don't need to have a stock of our titles. No unsold copies. Eliva Press uses environment friendly print on demand technology that limits the needs of publishing business. We care about environment and share these principles with our customers.
-Cover design. Cover art is designed by a professional designer.
-Worldwide distribution. We continue expanding our distribution channels to make sure that all readers have access to our books.

www.elivapress.com

www.ingramcontent.com/pod-product-compliance
Lightning Source LLC
Chambersburg PA
CBHW041152050326
40690CB00001B/451